MW01289617

THE PATH OF INTIMACY

*Your Guide to a Marriage
Filled with Passion and
Connection*

Scott Means

Published by HMM Creations LLC
4850 Sugarloaf Parkway Suite 209-183
Lawrenceville, GA 30044
resources@heavenmademarriage.com

Copyright © 2018 Scott Means
Cover Design and Illustrations © 2018 Scott
Means, HMM Creations LLC

All rights reserved. No part of this publication may be reproduced or transmitted in any form or by any means, including informational storage and retrieval systems, without permission in writing from the copyright holder, except for brief quotations in a review.

All Scripture quotations, unless otherwise indicated, are taken from the Holy Bible, New International Version®, NIV®. Copyright ©1973, 1978, 1984, 2011 by Biblica, Inc.™ Used by permission of Zondervan. All rights reserved worldwide. www.zondervan.com The "NIV" and "New International Version" are trademarks registered in the United States Patent and Trademark Office by Biblica, Inc.™

HMM Creations LLC
Lawrenceville, GA

Dedication

To my cherished bride, Jenni—my inspiration, my collaborator, my constant encourager, and my one true love.

Acknowledgements

To my darling wife. Thanks for dreaming with me, for believing when I have doubted, for keeping me moving forward when I felt stalled, and for the countless hours you contributed to this project and to the ministry we share.

To my many fellow marriage bloggers and ministers who steadfastly fight for couples and their marriages every day. Many of you have become friends on this journey, and many more of you have served to inspire, inform, and encourage me with your dedication, wit, and wisdom.

To Chris Taylor, Lifespring Writing, for her tremendous editing work and invaluable improvements in the clarity and accuracy of the text.

To all my readers, especially those of you who have shared with me the joys, questions, and struggles of your own marriages. You are the reason I do what I do.

Table of Contents

INTRODUCTION

Maybe you haven't ever said it out loud, but you have probably thought it. "There must be more to marriage than this."

In my more than 15 years of writing, teaching, and studying about marriage, one truth stands out above all the rest: almost everybody wants more for their marriage than they are currently experiencing. And there is one thing couples are looking for more than anything else: intimacy.

Whether we call it intimacy or connection or closeness, in survey after survey that I've done over the years, I've found that couples yearn for more of it. No matter the age, the number of years of marriage, the presence or absence of kids at home, or previous marital status, intimacy consistently rises to the top as people's biggest marital longing.

Hardwired

We were created by God with an innate desire for intimacy. We are made in His image, and just as God longs for connection with us, so too we have an innate desire for connection with Him, even if we don't recognize it as such.

This hardwired need for intimacy shows up in marriage, too, as my research and experience have shown. It's something couples are clamoring for, but few know how to get it.

In this book, you'll find help and hope for reigniting the intimacy in your marriage. In fact, I'll make a bold claim right here at the outset: You can have as much intimacy in your marriage as you want. I intend to show you how to get it.

I'll make a second claim, too: there is always more.

Regardless of how deeply connected to your spouse you feel, there is always a deeper level available to you than what you have right now. There is more fiery passion, a deeper level of connection, and more fun, adventure, and friendship than you are experiencing today.

The journey into deeper intimacy never ends.

The Pain of Marital Drift

Our deep-seated need for intimacy is why disconnection in marriage, our most important and intimate relationship, is so painful.

Yet so often we drift away from our spouse without realizing it. When left to inertia and natural human tendencies, intimacy will decline. It just doesn't happen on its own. This is why so many couples seem to wake up one day suddenly asking themselves questions like: "Where has the passion gone?" or "Why does he always treat me like that?" or "Why doesn't she trust me?" or "Why does he leave everything to me?" or "Does she always have to be such a nag?" or "Isn't she attracted to me anymore?"

My hope for your marriage and my goal for this book is to have you waking up and saying something different. Instead of questioning your marital intimacy, I want you to say things like, "Wow, I didn't know it could be this good after all these years," or "I can't believe we are still so in love," or "This just keeps getting better and better," or "I'm so thankful I am married to my best friend," or "You are the best thing that ever happened to me," or "No one else has what we have."

Two Paths

It is important to understand that intimacy is organic; it is a living thing. As such, it is either growing or dying. Very few living things can stay dormant for very long and survive. The same is true of the intimacy in your marriage.

You are either growing toward each other or growing away from each other as a couple. I describe this dynamic as a couple either being either on the **Path of Intimacy** or the **Path of Separation**. Make no mistake: you are on one or the other.

It takes a conscious effort to get on and stay on the Path of Intimacy, whereas the Path of Separation is easy to enter and even easier to stay on. We'll cover a lot more about these two paths in Chapters 5 and 6. You'll discover how to avoid the on-ramps to the Path of Separation and how to successfully navigate the Path of Intimacy.

Our Story

My wife and I have always had what I consider to be a good marriage. Even though we don't have a tragic marriage story, about fifteen years ago (some twenty years into our now 35-year marriage), I had a vague sense that God had something more for us in our marriage.

To get a better grasp my role as a husband, I embarked on a season of intense personal Bible study on the topic of marriage. I read every Bible passage I could find about marriage. Also, I began reading all the marriage books I could get my hands on. (I'm still somewhat of a marriage book junkie – you should see my Kindle!)

The season of seeking awakened me to God's passion for marriage. I came to understand the Bible as a love story. I saw in this story that God would go to any length to pursue intimacy with the people He created, including sending His own Son to a cruel death. So great was His desire for intimacy with us that He sent Jesus to be our Bridegroom in order to win us as His bride.

As my eyes were opening, suddenly everywhere I looked in my relationship with Jesus, I saw lessons for my marriage. This was exactly how God set it up, of course. He designed marriage to be a direct reflection of the relationship between Christ and Church. I came to understand that this isn't just a trite saying. Instead, it is the very key to marriage done well. It is the key to a passionate and intimate marriage. This understanding is what I and others refer to as the **Bridal Paradigm**: seeing my marriage through the lens of my relationship with Jesus.

I began to pursue my wife in the same relentless way Jesus pursues me. I began to try to love her with the same kind of intense and unstoppable love He lavishes on me.

Jenni, for her part, began to see our marriage through the truth of the Bridal Paradigm as well, leaning into my love and leadership as she did with Jesus. She began to open herself up more fully to me than she ever had before.

Thus began the long-term transformation process in our marriage that put us on the Path of Intimacy, which we continue on to this day. Many of the keys Jenni and I have discovered about staying on the Path of Intimacy are what you will find in the pages of this book.

CHAPTER 1: EXCELLENT ROOMMATES

"We are psychologically, emotionally, cognitively, and spiritually hardwired for connection, love, and belonging, and it is what gives purpose and meaning to our lives."[i]

Dr. Brene' Brown
Daring Greatly

The movie *Date Night* perfectly portrays a marriage that is stuck in the daily grind of real life. Claire and Phil have lost the passion they once had, having descended into a date night routine of going to the same restaurant, dining on the same meal, and having the same conversations every week. Although each of them is secretly longing for something more, something richer and deeper, they are bored and stuck in their routines.

They are issued a sudden wake-up call when their best friends, Brad and Haley, shock them with the news of their impending divorce. Brad confides in Phil that there is really nothing wrong with their marriage; they were fine but had just become excellent roommates. As Phil sadly relates this to Claire, he asks, "That's not what we are, is it?" "No," she says tentatively, then after a pregnant pause asks, "right?" Neither of them seems sure.

The rest of the movie comically portrays Claire and Phil's attempts to pump life back into their relationship through what evolves into a date night turned misadventure. The subplot, however, is that each of them tries to break out of their old habits of neglecting each other and their marriage.

Ultimately, the movie shows that Claire and Phil no longer settle for being excellent roommates. The closing lines of the movie:

> *Phil Foster: I'd do it again, you know?*
> *Claire Foster: What, tonight? No, it was very dangerous!!*
> *Phil Foster: No, not tonight. Us. You, me, the kids, all of it. I'd do it again. I'd choose you every time.*

The Goal of Your Marriage

The movie clearly portrays a couple who is adrift, slowly growing apart from each other, and seemingly unsure of what to do to breathe new life into their relationship. They have lost sight of the goal of their marriage.

What would you say is the most important goal of *your* marriage?

It's an important question. If you don't know the goal, you are more than likely thrashing around somewhat aimlessly, much as Phil and Claire were, without any real sense of purpose, direction, or destiny.

So, stop right here and think about it: What is the most important goal of *your* marriage?

Your answer to this question will significantly impact your marriage every day.

- - - -

Some may say marriage is primarily about their own happiness. Some say it's about leaving a legacy through their children. Some say companionship or friendship is of utmost importance. Some seek security or financial advantage. Others simply say the goal of marriage is to stay married.

While all of these have some truth to them, there is a singular goal for any and every marriage that ranks above all the others: intimacy.

Intimacy is the ultimate goal in marriage because intimacy is Jesus's ultimate goal in having us as His bride. There's a common belief that salvation through forgiveness of sins was the goal, but I don't look at it that way. Sin was the problem that separated us from God. Grace through Christ was the method God used to wipe out the sin. But God's ultimate goal was to live in intimate relationship with us, both now and forever, as His eternal bride.

Romans 12:2 says of Jesus:

> *"For the joy set before him he endured the cross, scorning its shame, and sat down at the right hand of the throne of God."*

What was the joy that enabled Jesus to leave heaven, to step into our human existence, and to sacrifice His very life for us before returning to the right hand of the Father? It was the joy of dwelling in intimacy with you and me – now and forever. Jesus wanted us so much that He laid down His life to have us.

What Is Intimacy?

Making intimacy the main goal of your marriage will change everything. But what exactly is intimacy?

In the next chapter, we will dive more deeply into understanding what intimacy is and what it is not. For now, let me put forward my definition:

Intimacy is being fully known and completely loved.

Being fully known makes it clear that intimacy is more than a euphemism for sex. It's more than an emotionally close feeling or having a marriage that is full of romance. For intimacy to reach its pinnacle, it must involve the entirety of your being: spiritual, emotional, and physical. It even extends to the financial, intellectual, and recreational dimensions of your marriage.

Genuine intimacy comes from knowing each other in every dimension of your beings and each of you responding to what you see with total and unconditional love.

We'll see in a later chapter how this deep level of intimacy in your entire beings does not imply at all that you and your spouse are the same. No, the beauty of intimacy is the way in which you can each bring your unique individual natures to the marriage union without losing who you are. In fact, the best marriages are ones in which each of you can walk fully in your true nature alongside each other, yet as one.

The Cost of Separation

There are many reasons that intimacy ceases to thrive in a marriage, a state that I describe as being on the Path of Separation. I use the term path because it rarely happens in an instant. It's not like falling off a cliff. It's more like getting lost in the woods. A couple loses sight of their goal (intimacy) and begins drifting until one day they realize they have wandered far down the path and are miles apart.

Regardless of how you got there, you'll soon discover that there is a serious cost to yourself and your marriage. The Path of Separation creates an ongoing sense of frustration as each of you feels the weight of your unmet needs. Loneliness often creeps in eventually. You may experience an underlying sense of guilt, knowing your marriage isn't what it should be and that you are likely a contributing factor. Alternatively, you might blame your spouse for your marriage woes. When you sense your spouse's disappointment and/or disapproval, you will react either with blame or shame. Fear can overtake you when you start to believe that your marriage is beyond recovery.

If you are experiencing any or all of these in your marriage, let me make it perfectly clear that no marriage, regardless of the reasons for being on the Path of Separation or how long you been there, is beyond redemption and recovery. It's never too late to get back on the Path of Intimacy. And, as we'll see in Chapter 6, it's not as hard as you might think.

Why Intimacy Matters

Intimacy in marriage matters because God is passionate about it. He understands that it is the most essential ingredient to your relationship with your spouse (and to your relationship with Him). He also hardwired you and me for intimacy. It is the key not only to making your marriage sustainable for the long haul, but to also making it full of all the passion, pleasure, and playfulness God intends for your marriage.

Intimacy is what keeps you and your spouse from settling for being excellent roommates.

CHAPTER 2:
UNDERSTANDING
INTIMACY

*"Therefore, a man shall leave his
father and mother and be joined
to his wife, and they shall become
one flesh. And they were both
naked, the man and his wife, and
were not ashamed."*[ii]

Genesis 2:24-25 (NKJ)

Let me briefly summarize the main points regarding intimacy in marriage that I've made so far:
1. Intimacy is the main goal of every marriage.
2. Most couples are desperate for more intimacy in their marriage.
3. The intimacy in your marriage is either growing or declining.
4. You can have as much intimacy as you want
5. It's never too late to work on the intimacy in your marriage.

The next step in our exploration of intimacy is to gain a solid understanding of what it is (and what it is not). We'll start by exploring the definition of intimacy that I gave in the previous chapter: intimacy is being fully known and completely loved.

In the creation story of Genesis, there is an extremely important yet frequently overlooked verse. Here, in the garden, in the very first marriage, before mankind's fall into sin, we see God's ideal intention for the interaction between man and woman:

> *"Therefore, a man shall leave his father and mother and be joined to his wife, and they shall become one flesh. And they were both naked, the man and his wife, and were not ashamed."*

Genesis 2:24-25 (NKJ)

Many quote Genesis 2:24, but leave off verse 25. In truth, these two verses are inseparable.

Naked and unashamed is how God meant us to live, and it has less to do with clothing or sex than you might think. Don't shortchange these verses by limiting them to the sexual union between husband and wife. While sex is one (very important) implication of being one and being naked, there is much more meaning here than that.

Being fully known and completely loved is, in essence, being naked and yet without shame. This is how marriage was meant to be from the beginning.

Fully Known – Getting Naked

Being fully known requires transparency in marriage, and transparency requires a willingness to be nakedly vulnerable. The degree of intimacy you share in your relationship will be capped by the degree of transparency and vulnerability you are willing to embrace.

The other implication of being *fully* known is that it must include all of you. And by all, I mean everything–even those areas where you feel bad about yourself.

Revealing all to your spouse means that along with your positive attributes, you expose your weaknesses, fears, and failures. Transparency is hard and requires a willingness to show the things you would rather hide from your spouse. We don't want to show the stuff we aren't proud of, mainly because of pride and fear. Because of pride, we don't want our spouse to think less of us. We fear that they will judge us. Ultimately, we fear that we will not be loved and accepted; we fear that we will be left disconnected.

Revealing all also includes our hopes, dreams, and ambitions, not just our fears and failures. It includes our shining victories and not just our defeats. In fact, intimacy grows deepest when we intentionally share these positive dimensions of our inner self because these best represent our true self.

Being fully known means allowing your spouse into every dimension of your being. As we'll see in the next section, many couples fail to embrace the all-encompassing nature of intimacy. Intimacy does not stop at the bedroom door. It doesn't stop at date night. It doesn't stop with having a deep spiritual connection. **Genuine intimacy excludes nothing.**

The nature of intimacy is that all the parts are interconnected. Sexual, emotional, spiritual, financial, intellectual, recreational, and more all feed off of each other. If you see a lack in one area, look at the degree of transparency and acceptance in the others. Are there areas where you are withholding yourself from your spouse? Are there areas where you are less than "fully in"?

Completely Loved - Without Shame

The second half of my intimacy definition, "completely loved," gets to the heart of the shame part of "naked without shame."

Where there is unconditional love, shame is replaced by acceptance and freedom.

Shame is the painful emotion caused by an overwhelming sense of guilt, embarrassment, and unworthiness. Shame drives us to hide and inhibits transparency. Shame destroys intimacy in marriage.

Shame is a powerful human emotion. Shame will cause us either to *accuse* ourselves or to *excuse* ourselves by blaming another, neither of which is helpful. Shame can keep a marriage trapped in fear, distrust, and secrecy. So how do we let go of shame?

Grace is the answer to shame's accusations. Grace is an invitation to intimacy. Grace says, "I love you completely. I see you, warts, weaknesses and all, and yet my love for you is undaunted." Grace says, "I choose to love you unconditionally because that's how God loves me."

We were made in the image of God; we were made for love and connection.

You see, shame has to do with *disgrace*, but love has to do with *grace*. To live in shame is to live in *darkness*, hiding in the shadows, but love allows us to live in the *light*, out in the open. Shame leads to dishonor, doubt, and fear, but love leads to confidence, delight and a sense of honor.

Fostering an Atmosphere of Grace

When you reveal yourself to your spouse, how can you guarantee that he or she will respond with unconditional love and grace?

You can't.

You only get to control your side of the equation, which is opening yourself up to your spouse and allowing yourself be seen.

Likewise, you can't make your spouse open up to you; that is their responsibility. You only get to control your response when it happens, which should be to show the same kind of love and grace you would like to receive.

When you choose the path of love and grace, you are choosing the Path of Intimacy, and two things will result. First, you will make it easier for your spouse to "get naked" with you. Second, you will shift the atmosphere of your marriage toward grace, which makes it more likely that your spouse will respond in kind.

Here are a few ideas that help to foster an atmosphere of grace in your marriage:

- It is unconditional, sacrificial love that makes way for us to be free of shame, despite our weakness and failings. Believe that love is at the core of all your spouse says and does, even when it doesn't always appear that way. Give them the benefit of the doubt.
- Grace should be offered generously and received thankfully. Learn to see yourself and your spouse through the eyes of Christ. Learning to see from heaven's perspective is what enables grace to flow freely.
- Never, ever use shame to manipulate or punish each other. It never really gets you what you want anyway. Shame always separates.
- Desire intimacy with your spouse more than you desire their perfection. Realize that condemnation puts you quickly onto the Path of Separation. Deal with issues in a way that preserves the connection with your spouse.
- Keep the Bridal Paradigm in mind. Consider how would Jesus respond, and try to offer a Christlike response to each situation. Remember how Jesus's highest priority is your heart, not your behavior.

What Real Couples Say about Intimacy

One dictionary defines intimacy as "a close, familiar, and usually affectionate or loving personal relationship with another person or group." [iii] When I read that, I thought, *Blah! Surely there must be more to it than that!*

So, I decided to ask the readers of my blog to define it for me. As not to constrain or lead the answers, I decided to use a simple, open-ended question. "What is Intimacy?" [iv] The potential problem I could foresee was that there was such a diversity of opinion about intimacy. If you ask a dozen people what intimacy is, you'll get thirteen answers. Maybe more.

Or so I used to think.

When I posted the "What is Intimacy?" question on my blog and got 75 responses, I expected the answers to be all over the place. It turns out I was wrong. All of the answers fell neatly in line with one of nine common answers, and most were bundled around just six common themes. I also expected a huge difference in the way men and women described intimacy. I was wrong there too. Or at least there was not as much difference as I had expected. There was one notable exception, which I'll get to later.

Most of those who responded to my question pointed to one of the three main areas of intimacy: physical/sexual, emotional/relational, or spiritual. About one in four included all three (physical, emotional, and spiritual) in their definitions.

As you might expect, slightly more men than women described intimacy in sexual terms, although the difference was not as large as I would have thought. Surprisingly, more men than women also included the emotional and spiritual dimension of intimacy in their answers.

Almost half of the respondents used words like closeness and connection when describing intimacy. Such answers tied with sexual intimacy in overall popularity.

As part of the poll, I also asked people to rank how satisfied they were with the intimacy in their marriage based on how they had just described it. Those who were most satisfied were those who described intimacy with terms like closeness and connection.

What about those who were least satisfied? That leads me to the most important finding from the survey.

The Transparency Difference

As I said, the differences in answers between men and women were all less than 10%, with one significant exception. The number one most popular answers for women (by far) included terms like vulnerability, openness, and transparency. By a three-to-one margin, more women than men identified this as a key component of intimacy.

And the least satisfied of all respondents were those who described intimacy as requiring transparency and vulnerability, the majority of whom were wives.

Based on my non-scientific blog poll, and backed up by years of talking about marriage with a diverse group of couples, I would say a significantly higher percentage of wives than husbands feel the need for transparency to foster intimacy in their marriage.

I attribute this male/female difference to two key factors. First, many men see transparency and vulnerability as a weakness (though the truth is it requires great strength) or unmanly. This is especially true when it comes to divulging weaknesses, fears, and failures—the ugly stuff men tend to want to hide from the world, and especially from the person from whom they want approval the most—their wives.

Second, transparency and vulnerability are most often communicated verbally. By-and-large, women tend to be better, or at least more frequent verbal communicators (of course, this is not universally true).

The answers to the "How satisfied are you with the intimacy in your marriage?" question indicate that the transparency difference between men and women is a crucial one.

In my survey, 61% of husbands were mostly or completely satisfied with the intimacy in their marriage as compared to only 43% of wives. Most of this difference can be attributed to the "missing piece" of vulnerability that most husbands have when it comes to intimacy.

The overall result I drew from asking how satisfied people were with the intimacy in their marriage is that on average people were only somewhat satisfied. And there was almost no variation in the average whether a couple was married two years or more than 30. That leaves lots of room for improvement!

CHAPTER 3: DON'T BUY THESE LIES

*"For if you embrace the truth, it will release more freedom into your lives."*ᵛ

Jesus
John 8:32 (TPT)

There are some common misconceptions about intimacy in marriage that will do damage if you believe them.

Don't buy the lies! Choose instead to embrace the truth.

Lie #1: Guys Don't Do Intimacy

In his book *Scary Close*, Donald Miller has a chapter about men and intimacy. He says, "I don't think men are as bad at intimacy as we might think. It's just that we get pressured to go about intimacy in ways that are traditionally more feminine, specifically we're asked to talk about it and share our feelings. We don't really want to do that." He goes on to say, "I think men do intimacy differently and I think that's okay."

In that same chapter, he also says, "The problem is most men are actually great at intimacy it's just that we've been led to believe we aren't. And I'm convinced the confusion is costing us."[vi]

I agree with Miller's assertion. Men do intimacy; they just do it differently than women. For many men, the path for emotional connection leads through the bedroom. A strong sexual connection makes them desire (not just be open to) a strong emotional connection. Another difference is that men tend to share more about facts and data than about their emotions because these are things that are important to them. Finally, men tend to use a lot fewer words than women do.

What all this points to is the fact that when it comes to intimacy (being fully known and totally loved and accepted), men approach it from a very different angle than women. We need to accept that difference in each other and be okay with it.

Truth: Your spouse probably does emotional intimacy differently than you do, and that's okay.

Lie #2: Sexual Intimacy Is For Him

It's amazing to me how many women believe this lie. Many women who don't have the same testosterone-laden sex drive as their husbands do think they are fine without sex. They aren't.

Sex is the only form of intimacy that God strictly reserved to be shared between husbands and wives, which makes sex not only unique but also sacred. In a Sexual Satisfaction Survey that I ran on my blog a few years back,

I found that one in five marriages are essentially sexless (defined as having sex less than once a month). A 2003 Newsweek article[vii] similarly reported psychologists' estimates that 15-20 percent of couples have sex fewer than ten times per year.

That is tragic.

Believing that sex is primarily for husbands will rob wives of the sexual enjoyment and fulfillment that God intends. It steals the oneness that is found in each other's arms. Further, because sex is the ultimate vulnerability in marriage, doing it only for your husband will cause you to miss out on the chance to be vulnerable with each other.

Sex is not primarily a physical act. It is deeply spiritual and builds a wide pathway to a strong emotional connection as well. Having sex regularly strengthens your marriage, gives you a sense of well-being, and it can help you actually desire sex more.

Truth: Don't let the fact that you may have less physical drive allow you to miss out on the joy and pleasure that is rightfully yours.

Lie #3: Spiritual Intimacy Is Less Important Than Other Kinds of Intimacy

The first two lies covered the emotional and sexual dimension of intimacy. There is also a lie we believe around the third area of intimacy, spiritual intimacy. That lie is that spiritual intimacy is less important than the other two.

Many couples work hard at maintaining emotional and sexual intimacy, but the truth is that spiritual intimacy is just as important to your marriage as the other two areas, if not more so. I've found that I can love my wife best when I am strongly connected to God. To be a good husband, I must first learn to be a bride—the much-loved bride of Christ. Further, when I am nurturing a close personal walk with Jesus, it allows my wife and me to share a deep spiritual connection.

I've observed that for many couples, the wife tends to gravitate more naturally and easily toward spiritual matters. However, God desires an intimate relationship with both husbands and wives. Husbands who leave the spiritual matters to their wives will miss out on the satisfaction and enjoyment that comes from leading their families spiritually. And because many wives desire for their husbands to have a thriving spiritual life, when a husband presses fully into his relationship with Jesus, it will deepen the intimacy in his marriage in the spiritual domain.

Truth: A thriving relationship with Jesus is for both husbands and wives and is the very foundation of a strong and intimate marriage.

Lie #4: Intimacy Needs to Be Earned

There is a natural tendency in marriage to withhold the intimacy your spouse desires until you feel your own intimacy needs are being met. While it's natural, it's a dangerous game that will quickly land your marriage on The Path of Separation, where you slowly spiral apart from each other.

The fact is that when you got married, the two of you became one. (See the next chapter for more about the stunning implications of this truth.) Therefore, intimacy should be your expectation at all times, and you'll want to continually and intentionally cultivate it. When you withhold intimacy, for whatever reason, you damage your connection and tear at the fabric of your oneness.

Withholding love and punishing your spouse for what you are not getting typically results in the opposite of what you hope it will accomplish. Waiting for your spouse to change before you become generous at meeting their needs does not invite him or her to move toward you. Rather, it pushes him or her away.

The best way to keep your marriage on the Path of Intimacy is for you to work on you and become the best husband or wife you can be.

Truth: Grace, not judgment, is the best path to an intimate marriage.

Lie #5: My Spouse Isn't on Board, So It's Hopeless

It's not easy when you feel as if you are the one doing all the giving in your relationship. It can be discouraging, especially if you've been in a long season where the relationship has felt one-sided. Still, let me encourage you to keep on loving well and not to make seeing changes in your spouse a prerequisite for love.

In most of the marriage transformation stories I've heard, including my marriage, change started with one spouse or the other. In my experience, someone has to go first. You might wish it to be otherwise, but since you can't control or change your spouse, your only option is for you to go first.

God calls us to love each other sacrificially and unconditionally, as He does. I believe that call is especially strong in marriage because I believe that love and grace are the forces most likely to transform your marriage. It isn't easy to focus more on giving than getting, but it is God's way.

Pray for your spouse to be awakened to love. Pray for your own heart to remain tender and open to the leading of the Holy Spirit where your marriage is concerned. Pray hopefully and expectantly for God to move in your heart, in your spouse's heart, and in your marriage.

Truth: Continuing to walk in love and grace is your best hope for a transformed marriage.

Lie #6: It's Too Late For Us

If your marriage has spent a long time on the Path of Separation, it can feel like there is no chance of getting onto the Path of Intimacy.

You think to yourself, "Our habits are too ingrained. We drifted too far apart. This is just unrecoverable." But these are lies. While there are no guarantees, I believe that no marriage is beyond hope. I've heard it said that there are no hopeless marriages, only hopeless people.

God is a redeemer by nature, and He is for your marriage. He longs for it to be all you dream of. He longs for it to be all *He* dreams of.

It's never too late to step off the Path of Separation and onto the Path of Intimacy. It doesn't matter what state our marriage is in or how long it's been there. In Chapters Five and Six you'll learn some practical steps to reversing course.

Truth: It's never too late to get back on the Path of Intimacy.

Lie #7: I Don't Have Time or Energy for This

It's true that busyness and exhaustion are big enemies of marital intimacy. It's especially difficult for couples with young children to find ways to foster connection. It feels much of the time like there is nothing left for each other.

Getting on the Path of Intimacy starts with a change in mindset. Thinking differently about your spouse, your marriage, and your role in it requires discipline, but it doesn't necessarily require a lot of time and energy. It's primarily about learning to be watchful for opportunities to express love in small ways on a daily basis. We'll dig deeper into the concept of Watchfulness in Chapter 10.

Many couples, especially when in a season of stress and busyness, figure they can put their marriage on hold until later. The problem is that later often never comes. Or when later does come, they find that the intimacy in their marriage has dissolved completely. Although it's never too late to get back on the Path of Intimacy, don't waste valuable years of your marriage stuck in separation and sadness.

I tell couples all the time, "It's the little things." And it's true. Intimacy can be fostered by being known and being loved in small ways.

It's okay to let yourself be known even when you are tired and burned out. In fact, it's even more important in those seasons, because it enables you and your spouse to bear one another's burdens.

And making your husband or wife feel loved is mostly a matter of knowing how he or she wishes to be loved and then finding little ways to show love in that way every day.

Truth: Maintaining the intimacy in your marriage is mostly about doing the little things.

CHAPTER 4: YOU REALLY ARE ONE

"'For this reason a man will leave his father and mother and be united to his wife, and the two will become one flesh.' This is a profound mystery—but I am talking about Christ and the church."[viii]

Ephesians 5:31-32 (NKJ)

Want to know an awesome secret? You and your spouse are one. It's true.

How do I know? Because the covenant of marriage works the same as our covenant with Jesus. When we come to faith in Him, we become one with Him (1 Corinthians 6:17). In the same way, when you entered into marriage, you and your spouse became one.

"'For this reason a man will leave his father and mother and be united to his wife, and the two will become one flesh.' This is a profound mystery—but I am talking about Christ and the church."

Ephesians 5:31-32 (NKJ)

It's mysterious and wonderful, yet the intention couldn't be clearer. A husband and wife are joined together in the same way we are joined to Christ. Oneness is literally a mega-mystery, as Paul states. .

How would you live and love differently if you really believed that you and your spouse are one?

Unpacking the Mega-Mystery

The first thing to realize about the whole two-become-one mystery is that it is not something you do.

It's not even something you grow into. It's something you **are**.

You **are** one. The Bible declares it to be so.

Yeah, I know, it's hard to get your head around that sometimes because so often it doesn't *feel* that way, right? I mean we fight, we get self-absorbed, and sometimes we allow ourselves to drift apart. We head down the Path of Separation. How can I say you are one through all of that?

That's the mystery. You are one with your spouse by virtue of the fact that you chose to marry each other. It's that simple.

To make this notion a little clearer, let me draw the spiritual parallel to which Paul alludes to in Ephesians. As believers, we are one with Christ whether we "feel" one or not. How we feel is not the issue. The oneness we share with Him gives us access to all kinds of great things like a 24/7 intimate walk with Christ, the continuing fellowship of the Holy Spirit, the same power that raised Jesus from the dead, the right to ask anything in Jesus' name, etc.

Whether or not we tap into all these great fruits of our oneness does not change the fact that we are one with Christ.

Enjoying the Fruit of Oneness

If you are already one with your husband or wife, then it is kind of silly for you to "try" to be one. The question isn't really how to become one. The question is how do we fully enjoy the fruit of the oneness that is already ours just because we are married?

What are the implications of our oneness in marriage?

Score-keeping

Score-keeping comes about when we attempt to compare what we *get* from our spouse to what we *give*. It can come into play in many areas such as household chores and finances. However, the most deadly kind of scorekeeping is when it comes to having our needs met.

Because you are one, these kinds of score-keeping comparisons make absolutely no sense. Our oneness means that when my wife "wins," then so do I. It's either win-win or lose-lose.

Self

Likewise, self-centeredness, self-protection, self-promotion, and self-reliance have no place in light of the fact that we are one. Oneness means we shift our thinking from me-centered to we-centered. It's no longer a matter just of what is best for me, but what is best for us, and consequently what is best for my spouse.

When I choose to meet my wife's needs, I'm actually also helping myself. When I hurt my wife, I'm actually hurting myself.

Intimacy

Intimacy in all forms (spiritual, physical, emotional, intimacy, financial, and intellectual) is the intended state of my marriage because my wife and I are one. Though oneness is not the same as intimacy, oneness grants us free access to intimacy.

I don't need to "perform" or jump through certain hoops to earn intimacy with my wife, and she doesn't need to perform for me, either. Oneness gives us immediate access to intimacy by right.

Separation

When we choose the Path of Separation instead of the Path of Intimacy, we tear at the fabric of our oneness. Separation brings emotional pain because it is never intended to be our default state. Even when we are hurt or offended, choosing to separate is never the right path.

Complements

Neither of us is more or less; instead, we are a perfect complement to each other. We are two who have become fully one. Though we hold different roles in our marriage, we don't compete against each other but instead choose to serve each other.

Freedom

I am completely free to bring my full self to my marriage, to hold nothing back from my wife. Because we are one, hiding and withholding are inappropriate. I am fully hers, as she is fully mine.

Oneness Is Not Sameness

There is a common misunderstanding about what "two become one" means. Being one does not mean conforming yourself to your spouse. Rather, it means bringing the fullness of your true self, naked and unashamed, without fear, into your relationship for the benefit of your spouse and your marriage.

Being one does not mean thinking, feeling, and dreaming the same way as your spouse. Oneness does not mean sameness. Rather, intimacy happens when you bring the fullness of yourself, your thoughts, your feelings, your hopes, and your wishes to your marriage in a way that honors your spouse and his or her true nature, who God created them to be in their inner-most being.

Learn to affirm and value each other for who you really are rather than who you wish they would be for you. Celebrate and agree with heaven's perspective of your spouse.

One in Your Whole Being

In the previous chapter, we covered the fact that intimacy is multi-dimensional. In fact, it involves every dimension of your being and marriage. By extension, the same is true of being one.

Let's take a look how being one works out in three most commonly understood dimensions of our human existence: spirit, soul, and body.

Spirit

Your spirit (and your spouse's spirit) is the essence of your nature. It's the real you, as God created you to be. It is our human spirit that fellowships most readily with the Holy Spirit.

Being one in spirit with your spouse is about the extent to which you really "get" each other, how well you know each other in your innermost beings. This is critical, because we all sometimes think, act. and speak in ways that are inconsistent with our true God-breathed nature. In times like this, we have the opportunity to look past our spouse's behavior into the truth of who they are. We have the privilege of speaking grace and truth into their life. We get to have a front-row seat in what God is doing in and through our spouse and get to actively partner with the Holy Spirit to remind them who they are.

Soul

Your soul includes your mind, will, and emotions. It is your conscious existence.

Being one in the realm of the soul is what grants a couple access to emotional intimacy and other kinds of intimacy that have to do with our practical life (finances, intellect, etc.). We commonly hear a happy couple described as being "soul mates." To me, being soul mates is really about baring your soul (thoughts, feelings, hopes, and dreams) to your mate, about being totally transparent and vulnerable with each other. As I noted above, oneness of soul does not mean we have the same thoughts and emotions as our spouse, but it means we join our souls together in a mutually beneficial way.

Body

The body is the physical container for our spirit and soul and grants us access to the world through our senses.

Oneness of body clearly refers to our sexual union. That is the literal meaning of two becoming one flesh. Being one in body means that our physical bodies belong to each other, as the Bible explains in 1 Corinthians 7. We are to freely and unashamedly offer our physical bodies to one another for our mutual pleasure and satisfaction. As such, the bedroom (or wherever) is where being "naked and unashamed" takes on a literal meaning.

CHAPTER 5: WHY INTIMACY MATTERS MOST

*Observe how Christ loved us. His love
was not cautious but extravagant. He
didn't love in order to get something
from us but to give everything of
himself to us. Love like that.*[ix]

Ephesians 5:1-2 (The Message)

If we are already one, doesn't that mean that we already
have intimacy? Not really, as you'll see.

You see, oneness and intimacy are not the
same. Oneness is a state of *being*. You are one. Intimacy is
a state of *knowing and loving*. You have to pursue intimacy.

Relentlessly pursuing intimacy is the best way to fully
experience the benefits of two being one.

The Spiritual Parallel

The clearest way for me to explain how this works in
marriage is to examine the spiritual parallel in my
relationship with Jesus, through the lens of the Bridal
Paradigm.

An unseen spiritual oneness with Christ happens at
salvation. As we grow in intimacy with Him, our thoughts,

our emotions, and our will come into agreement with and yield to the Savior who indwells us by the working of the Holy Spirit in us. As we learn to walk more fully in the guidance and power of the Holy Spirit, our words and actions bear the fruit of the oneness we have with Jesus. "We know by this that He abides in us, by the Spirit whom He has given us" (1 John 3:24-NKJ)[x].

All of this flows out of fostering an intimate relationship with Jesus. Intimacy with Jesus comes in the same way as intimacy in marriage. Intimacy reaches its pinnacle when we allow ourselves to be fully known, nakedly transparent before God, and fully loved for who we are. Intimacy with Jesus brings to the point of full surrender of ourselves unto Him.

When I come to Jesus, naked and without shame, I experience the fullness of His unconditional love and unfathomable grace toward me. Then, as I get to know Jesus more intimately and deeply, my love for Him grows. He invites me in and encourages me to give over more of myself to Him. It is essentially Him being fully known and completely loved by me— my very definition of intimacy. (Of course, as in marriage, this "fully knowing" God is a lifelong pursuit that never ends.) There is an ongoing cycle of knowing more and loving more that grows the intimacy in my walk with Him.

To experience the vast riches God intends for our marriage, riches that are rightfully ours through the oneness we have in our marriage covenant, we must vigorously pursue intimacy with each other.

THE PATH OF INTIMACY

Intimacy must take the highest priority.

Love Like That

Paul prefaces his instructions on marriage in Ephesians 5 by encouraging us to examine how Christ loves us:

> *Watch what God does, and then you do it, like children who learn proper behavior from their parents. Mostly what God does is love you. Keep company with him and learn a life of love. Observe how Christ loved us. His love was not cautious but extravagant. He didn't love in order to get something from us but to give everything of himself to us. Love like that.*

Ephesians 5:1-2 (The Message)

We are called to "love like that" as a fundamental way of doing marriage. Selflessly. Extravagantly. Giving ourselves completely to one another, and holding nothing back.

It is in learning to "love like that" that we discover the secret to marital transformation. It is the surest way to attain the kind of intimacy, passion, and love you dream of.

That's a big promise, but one I believe in.

Why Intimacy Matters Most

How do I know that intimacy is what matters most in marriage?

In the Bridal Paradigm, which is my understanding of myself as the bride of Christ, God portrays the perfect picture of marriage. It is through that lens that I see Christ as my Bridegroom, a lover pursuing an eternal bride.

Contrary to what many think, Christ's pursuit of us, a pursuit that cost him his very life, was not so he could get us to follow all the religious rules. No, Jesus's pursuit of His bride was so we could live in intimacy with Him forever as his bride, starting right here and now. He is after relationship, not rules!

As our hearts are transformed by our relationship with Jesus, our response is to care about the things that are important to Him. It doesn't work the other way around. Just doing the right things doesn't lead to an intimate relationship.

Intimacy is the most important thing in marriage because intimacy is what matters most in my relationship with God. It's that simple.

The Endless Pursuit of Intimacy

It's simple, but it isn't easy.

I mean, if I really, truly grasped the importance of intimacy in my marriage, I would probably do a lot of things differently. You probably would, too. But it requires that we be intentional. And it requires that we never stop pursuing it.

Genuine intimacy in marriage doesn't happen on its own. The natural state of a relationship is not intimacy but coexistence. When left untended, a marriage can easily devolve over time into little more than being excellent roommates.

We all desire more intimacy in our marriage, but we don't always *do* the things that best build and maintain intimacy. We descend quickly onto the Path of Separation because we don't make choices that keep us on the Path of Intimacy.

If Intimacy Really Mattered Most...

If I put the goal of intimacy with my wife ahead of everything else in our relationship, a lot of things would have to change.

- I would no longer see having my personal needs met as the most important thing in our relationship. Instead of asking, "What can I get from her?" I would ask, "What can I do to maintain our connection?"

- I would not depend on my wife to make me happy and to keep me that way. Instead, I would find the greatest happiness when our intimacy is deepest. I would gladly take the lead in our pursuit of every form of intimacy.

- Demanding my rights and insisting on my "fair share" would be replaced by looking out for what is best for our marriage and for my wife.

- When I feel offended or disappointed, instead of reacting by keeping an emotional distance, I would press closer to her, seek to understand what is really going on, and do my best to eliminate whatever is standing between us. I would see maintaining our connection as more important than proving my case.

- Instead of giving my wife only my leftovers, after my job and ministry and chores have taken everything out of me, I would make sure I have sufficient physical, emotional, sexual, and mental energy to give the best part of me to her.

Of course, these examples apply to both husbands and wives. And each of these examples represents choices that will determine the course that the intimacy in our marriage will take: the Path of Separation or the Path of Intimacy.

To help you be mindful of such choices, consider the following principles concerning happiness in marriage.

1. The purpose of your marriage is not your own personal happiness.
2. You must own your own happiness.
3. You should lavish love on your spouse as if their happiness depends on you.

In the next two chapters, we will deal specifically and how the daily choices we make will either maintain and build the intimacy in our marriage or damage it.

CHAPTER 6: AVOIDING ON-RAMPS TO THE PATH OF SEPARATION

Do nothing out of selfish ambition or vain conceit. Rather, in humility value others above yourselves,

Philippians 2:3

We have established that due to the organic nature of intimacy, you are either growing toward each other or growing away from each other as a couple. You are either on the Path of Intimacy or the Path of Separation. There is no neutral path.

When left to inertia and natural human tendencies, intimacy tends to decline. It takes a conscious effort to get on and stay on the Path of Intimacy, whereas the Path of Separation is easy to enter and even easier to stay on.

The Path of Separation is often a subtle one. You may be on it for months or even years before you realize that your marriage lacks the kind of intimacy and passion you once had and the kind of intimacy and passion you desire. By then, the habits and patterns of thinking have become old and deeply ingrained, making it difficult to reverse course and get back on the Path of Intimacy. You believe you have fallen out of love.

Two things are true about the Path of Separation. First, the longer you are on it, the further you will grow apart. Second, the further you go, the faster the separation accelerates. The Path of Separation is a true downward spiral. Although there is always hope for recovery, the best thing for your marriage is to avoid it altogether.

In this chapter, we'll focus how to avoid the on-ramps that lead you down the Path of Separation.

On-Ramp #1: When Differences Are Ignored

If you don't think God has a sense of humor, consider the fact that He chose to join two such dramatically different creatures as men and women into one.

It may not be politically correct to say so, but it's an obvious fact is that men and women differ in all kinds of ways, and many of these differences work their way out on a daily basis in our marriages. In addition to the obvious physical differences in sexual organs, there are a few differences that have marital implications:[xi] [xii]

- Women have language processing centers on both sides of the brain, whereas men have them only on the left side. Also, men have fewer connections between verbal centers. Draw your own conclusions on that one.
- Women are more sensitive—literally. Their larger brain memory center, and the higher density of neural connection into it, means they have a better sense of smell and have more pain receptors.

- Men produce more of the hormone testosterone, which is associated with sex and aggression. In addition to the female reproductive hormone estrogen, women also produce more oxytocin, which is a bonding hormone.
- The higher blood flow in the brains of females will cause them to linger in thought or revisit emotional memories more than males, who tend to process a thought or emotion and move on.
- Male brains utilize nearly seven times more gray matter for activity while female brains utilize nearly ten times more white matter. This gives men an increased ability to focus on that task at hand and allows women a better ability to multi-task.
- Men's hearts are larger than women's (though not true in the figurative sense).
- Men have thicker skin (true also in the figurative sense).

One of the ways these physiological and psychological differences show up in marriage is that men and women tend to have very different priorities when it comes to their needs.

In another survey I did on my blog, I asked husbands and wives to answer this question: "What is the *one* thing you need most from your spouse?" I allowed only one answer. To make processing the data easier, I supplied a list of seven choices; I also allowed for write-in responses. Here are the results for husbands and wives, in priority order.

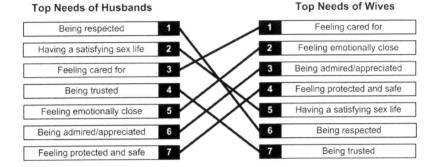

My informal findings are supported by other, more scientific studies and popularized by such books as *Men are From Mars, Women are From Venus*, by Dr. John Gray, and *His Needs, Her Needs* by Dr. Willard Harley. In *For Women Only*, author Shaunti Feldhahn concludes that respect and honor mean more to most husbands than love and affection. The companion book *For Men Only* describes the high priority wives place on feeling loved and pursued by their husbands.

The book *Love and Respect* by Emmerson Eggerichs is centered on the differing needs of men and women based on the passage of scripture found in Ephesians:

> *"However, each one of you also must love his wife as he loves himself, and the wife must respect her husband."*

Ephesians 5:33

The bottom line of all these differences between men and women is that it makes marriage pretty complicated.

One complication is that husbands and wives tend to misunderstand, or worse, overlook their partner's key needs. Because I'm wired so differently from my wife, it takes a significant effort to discern her needs and an even greater effort to figure out how to meet them in a way that is meaningful to her.

On-Ramp #2: When Needs Go Unmet

A second complication is that we tend to naturally give love in the same way we wish to receive it. Obviously, given the differences in needs between husbands and wives, this is a formula for much discord.

For example, one of my highest felt needs is for respect, which is a common need for husbands. My wife, on the other hand, has a high need for tender expressions of love. If I were to follow my natural inclination, I would make sure that my wife feels respected by me. Conversely, she would go out of her way to show me tender love expressions. The problem with this is obvious. Neither of us would receive what the other is giving as love because we speak a different love language.

This discussion about needs is critically important because having unmet needs is one of the quickest and most prominent on-ramps to The Path of Separation. Unmet needs lead to feelings of disappointment, resentment, and ultimately feeling unloved. All of this leads to disconnection.

Over time, each will become more focused on his or her own unmet needs than on the needs of the other, further aggravating the problem. It's like when you are starving, all you can think about is food. Eventually, if left unchecked, a couple will spiral down the Path of Separation, where one or both of the individuals in the marriage feels neglected, unloved and undesirable, becoming deeply dissatisfied and feeling emotionally isolated and lonely.

Here a few tips for avoiding the unmet needs on-ramp:

- Assume that your partner has different love needs than you do.
- Give love in the way your spouse likes to receive it, not like to receive it.
- Never stop being a student of your spouse, continually learning what delights him or her the most.

On-ramp #3: When It's All About You

I often describe the Path of Separation as the path of self, because selfishness, self-protection, and self-sufficiency all fight against genuine intimacy and present easy opportunities for a couple get disconnected.

It's not necessarily easy or natural to put our spouse's needs ahead of our own, but there is a clear biblical mandate to do so:

> *Do nothing out of selfish ambition or vain conceit. Rather, in humility value others above yourselves,*

> *Philippians 2:3*

The on-ramp of self will cause you to withhold yourself and your love from your spouse, only giving in the same proportion as you feel you are receiving. This is a death spiral.

Here are some typical ways husbands take the on-ramp of self:

- Acting disinterested in family matters and his wife's personal concerns, focusing instead on his work life and hobbies.
- Withdrawing emotionally when feeling disrespected or challenged.
- Refusing to make decisions, leaving the burden of decision-making to his wife.
- Acting in a self-obsessed or totalitarian manner that fails to properly consider his wife's desires.
- Failing to appreciate that his wife's need for romance never ends, even after years of marriage.
- Withholding emotional connection and affection in response to unmet sexual needs.
- Neglecting his role as spiritual head of the family.
- Withdrawing and giving up when she acts in a controlling manner.

Here are some typical ways wives take the on-ramp of self:

- Being critical or accusatory toward her husband, especially in front of others, when her needs go unmet or when he makes a mistake.

- Withholding sex or using it as a weapon in response to her unmet emotional needs.
- Continually battling for authority or contending for power. Not allowing him to lead in a way that allows him to feel respected.
- Retaliating by intentionally acting against his expressed wishes.
- Failing to appreciate his need for her overt expressions of sexual desire.
- Putting the children before her husband, or worse, treating him like a child.

It isn't easy to die to yourself and manage your expectations. It isn't natural to choose relationship and connection over our rights and desires. The way of selfless love can be hard, but it is the way that holds the greatest promise of intimacy.

When you focus on all the ways our spouse isn't measuring up and hold their shortcoming against them, your spouse will react by drawing away or lashing out defensively. No one will choose to move closer to someone who they feel is only judging them.

Here's a sure sign that judgment and resentment are ruling your marriage: you catch yourself saying "If my husband/wife would just _____ , our marriage would be so much better."

Here are just a few examples to illustrate what I'm talking about:

- A wife expects her husband to help more around the house and resents him when he doesn't.
- A couple tries to divide everything 50-50, and both are thinking it's more like 70-30 in their spouse's favor.
- A husband expects his wife to want sex as much as he does and expresses his disappointment to her routinely.
- A wife is critical of her husband's lack of handyman skills and compares him unfavorably to her father.
- A husband doesn't think his wife keeps things tidy enough for his liking, yet he refuses to lend a hand.
- A wife thinks her husband should learn to be more romantic and compares him negatively with the husbands of her friends (or of the latest romance novel she is reading).

In each of these situations, the husband's or wife's own needs and desires are at the heart of their thinking. These needs and desires are not bad in and of themselves, but when we put our individual needs ahead of our relationship and ahead of our spouse's needs, we start down the Path of Separation.

On-ramp #4: When You Push on the Rope

There is an object lesson I use when my wife and I teach our marriage small group. In the lesson, I lay a length of rope on the ground and ask for a volunteer. I then instruct the unsuspecting volunteer to try to move the rope by pushing on one end. Obviously, it doesn't work. The rope just bunches up into a mess. Then I ask the person to move the rope by pulling on the opposite end. Voila! The whole thing moves.

The saying I use is in this object lesson is that when it comes to meeting needs in marriage, "You can't push on a rope." Focusing mostly on getting your own needs met, and pushing your spouse to do so, is like pushing on a rope. It doesn't work, and you usually end up with a mess.

The same push/pull dynamic occurs when we try to change each other. The reality is that the only person you can change is you. It's pretty pointless to try to change your husband or wife. Instead, work on you—on becoming the best spouse you can be.

Demanding, cajoling, and manipulating your spouse often will result in the exact opposite of what you are trying to accomplish.

The remedy for this on-ramp is simply to focus more on what you give to your spouse than on what you get from him or her and to work on changing yourself more than you work on trying to change your spouse.

Spending time actively pursuing intimacy shifts the dynamic in your marriage from pushing to pulling.

On-ramp #5: When You Only Give Leftovers

Giving your spouse only what's left of you after you have given to your kids, your job, your church, and your social engagements is a sure way to land your marriage on the Path of Separation. Given how crazy-busy most of us are these days, when you don't reserve part of your time and energy for your spouse, there will almost certainly be nothing left for him or her.

You and your spouse are in a covenant relationship. You can only say that about two relationships in your life: your relationship with your spouse and your relationship with Jesus. That puts your marriage in a completely different category from your kids, job, church, friends, and other family members. That means you can't just put your spouse and marriage on your to-do list like everything else. You can't look at investing in your marriage as another task to be completed.

We tend to separate our lives into "spiritual" and "non-spiritual" categories, but the truth is, as Christ-followers, it's all spiritual. In a similar vein, because you and your spouse are one, there is nothing you do that is completely apart from your spouse, even when you are not physically doing it together.

Just as we walk with Jesus daily and abide in Him continually, we "walk with" our spouse. The first implication of this spiritual/marital parallel is that we have to prioritize one-on-one time together because that is the foundation of the intimacy we share. That one-on-one time has to be more than discussing schedules and to-do lists. In those times, to build deep connection, we also need to get real, to be transparent, and to let ourselves be seen. Also, we need to purposefully express love and allow ourselves to receive love.

The other implication of the spiritual/marital parallel is that we need to see everything we do in the light of our marriage and the relationship we have with our spouse. Just as in your relationship with Jesus, your marriage is an integral part of all that you are and do.

CHAPTER 7: STAYING ON THE PATH OF INTIMACY

Surrender is not burdensome but a joyful choice motivated by love.[xiii]

Johnathan David Helser

As important as it is to avoid the Path of Separation, as we learned in the previous chapter, it's even more important to deliberately steer your relationship onto the Path of Intimacy and to make every effort to keep it there.

If the Path of Separation is the path of *self,* then the Path of Intimacy is the path of *surrender.*

The Way of Surrender

Don't be fooled by the word surrender. Surrender in marriage has nothing to do with defeat, loss, or giving up. No, I use "surrendered marriage" to describe the kind of marriage revealed to us in the relationship between Christ and the church.

The English word "surrender" comes from two Anglo-Norman French words: sur and render. Let's break it down

1. **Sur** – a prefix meaning over and above. Think *sur*charge or *sur*tax, something you pay over and above regular charges or normal taxes.

2. Render – to give. To hand over. To abandon oneself entirely to.

Put these two together and what do you have? You have the very heart of marital surrender:

> *Surrender: To go over and above in giving yourself to your spouse and marriage.*

Surrender means being all in 100%, holding nothing back.

Surrender means complete transparency and vulnerability with each other.

Surrender is giving, not out of compulsion or duty but out of love and a desire to see your wife or husband thrive.

It is not giving to get. It's not a mindset of "I'll scratch your back, but you better scratch mine at least as much if not a little more." That is self-serving and manipulative. We are after unconditional love.

Surrender means giving to bless and giving to foster intimacy. It means learning what love looks like to your spouse and then doing that in the little things every day.

Surrender means giving your spouse what he or she needs from you – and then some. Try to out-give, out-bless, and out-love each other. That is the only kind of competition that belongs in a surrendered marriage.

Surrendering the Way of Self

A surrendered marriage calls us to surrender self.

A marriage built on surrender is one in which husband and wife are selfless and self-sacrificing instead of self-centered and self-satisfying. Surrender requires living against our human nature because our natural path is the path of self. Rather than focusing on the questions of "What are my rights?" and "What do I get out of this marriage?", we are instead to focus on "What can I give to benefit and bless my spouse?" and "What can I do to strengthen our marriage?"

The way of surrender calls us to care about the things your spouse cares about, even if they aren't things that would naturally matter to you. Surrender means maintaining a culture of honor in your home, attending to one another's needs, being willing to sacrifice your own desires in order to delight your wife or husband.

A surrendered marriage sets aside the notion that 50-50 compromise is the ideal and instead goes for 100-100, where each strives to give 100% to the other. Giving 100% of yourself calls you to bring your whole self, the good and the not so good, naked and unashamed, into your marriage. Each spouse brings his or her entire self, as the two of you are joined together in spirit, soul, and body. This is what it means for two to become one. You live as one flesh for the benefit of each other and your marriage.

In a surrendered marriage, husband and wife do not strive for equality but strive instead to outdo one another in loving, giving, and sacrificing. Score-keeping and competition give way to a new mindset that acknowledges the one-flesh nature of marriage. "When my wife wins so do I." "When my husband wins so do I."

The Mutual Surrender of Husband and Wife

Ephesians 5 beautifully describes how mutual surrender is to work in marriage as we strive to be a reflection of the love relationship between Christ and the church.

A husband's surrender primarily takes the form of loving, sacrificial leadership. He gives of himself fully to serve, protect, and provide for his wife and family as Christ does for the church. He invests himself in nurturing his wife's wellbeing, covering her spiritually, and doing all in his power to see her thrive in her full identity and reach her full potential. With Christ as his example, he is to love his wife unconditionally.

A wife's surrender primarily takes the form of leaning into her husband's loving leadership, giving herself fully to him as the church does to Christ. She honors him with the gifts of her respect and submission, supporting him and remaining under his protective covering not because she is incapable or inferior in any way but because she chooses to live within the ordered partnership that is God's design for marriage.

The key to a surrendered marriage is to pour yourself into fulfilling the things God has called you to in his Word and to put all your effort into meeting your spouse's needs. Don't worry about what the Bible calls your spouse to do or about pushing your spouse to meet your needs. Focus on your part rather than your spouse's part. What you will find is that when you fulfill your part, you make a wide pathway that invites your spouse to step more fully into theirs.

Focusing on your own issues and personal growth is what creates an atmosphere that invites rather than pushes your spouse to meet your needs. This is "pulling on the rope" rather than pushing on it. It works much better.

This kind of selfless, sacrificial love is what keeps your marriage on the Path of Intimacy.

The Upward Spiral of Knowing and Loving

The Path of Intimacy leads to fulfillment in your marriage relationship in an ongoing and evermore increasing fashion.

Remember, being known completely and loved absolutely is where intimacy reaches its pinnacle. Surrender says to one another, "Here I am—weakness, warts and all, but all I am is yours." Our only fitting response is, "I see you as you are, and I am completely in love with you. And I want to delight you."

An upward spiral in your relationship results from the ongoing cycle of being known and loved and knowing and loving.

It is what happens when your spouse sees you for who you are, understands your heart's desires, and not only shows you love and acceptance but also serves to meet your needs and deepest desires. When in a like manner you serve to meet the desires of your spouse's heart, they respond with the trust and transparency that allows them to be fully seen for who they are.

This cycle of being intimately known and understood and receiving a response of love, expressed in ways that meet your innermost needs, is the ultimate satisfaction of a marriage lived on the Path of Intimacy. The more you learn to love and surrender, the more love and surrender grow.

Real Love

When I describe responding to your spouse with love, I'm not talking about love only as an emotion or feeling.

Although love is partly an emotion, it is more so a decision of the will to think and act in accordance with your spouse's love needs. The amazing thing is that as you each begin to surrender your "rights" and focus on loving and serving each other, without expectations or demands for something in return, an amazing and delightful dynamic unfolds.

Real love is action. Real love makes daily choices to serve and surrender self. Real love does its best to out-love, out-give, out-serve, and out-surrender to one another. Real love also requires that you push yourself to go beyond doing the bare minimum; you do your part—and then some. Real love holds hold nothing back, surrendering yourself wholly to one another.

As you proceed down the Path of Intimacy, emotional love grows as a result. The fruits of passion, trust, pleasure, and freedom all grow along with it.

The Power of Pleasure

Pleasure is a power source that propels your marriage further along the Path of Intimacy as little else can.

Seek to find pleasure in your mate and to know with certainty that he or she finds equal pleasure in you. Of course, one important component of pleasure is sexual pleasure, but I'm talking about more than just keeping things passionate in the bedroom.

To successfully love each other selflessly over the long haul, you will have to get past the point of merely meeting each other's needs out of a sense that it's the right thing to do. You'll also learn to meet their needs— and then some, going beyond giving the bare minimum. Instead of seeing it as a duty, learn to take pleasure in loving one another lavishly, in delighting each other, and in giving and receiving pleasure in all forms: physically, emotionally, spiritually and intellectually.

Shift your mindset from "I need to" to "I want to," and ultimately to "I get to." Move from loving your spouse well out of a sense of duty to loving him or her well because it is a privilege.

A surrendered marriage enhances intimacy not only because you dig deeply into each other and find delight in what you discover there, but also because as you learn what delights and gives pleasure to one another, you make delight and pleasure a high priority.

It's not always easy to live in the place of delight in each other, especially among the daily pressures of life. There will be plenty of mundane existence in between joyous flashes of pleasure. In the final chapter, we will examine how the principle of watchfulness can help you seek more opportunities to take pleasure in and give delight to your spouse.

CHAPTER 8: TRAIL MARKERS ON THE PATH OF INTIMACY

"If you can find a path with
no obstacles, it probably
doesn't lead anywhere." [xiv]

Frank A. Clark

Over the course of my life, I have hiked a significant portion of the Appalachian Trail (the 2200-mile long East Coast trail that runs from Georgia to Maine). If you spend much time hiking that trail at all, you immediately come to depend on the white "blazes" that clearly (and sometimes not so clearly) mark the trail. They keep you on the right path.

That's the intent of this chapter: to give you practical markers to use to keep your relationship on the Path of Intimacy.

To this point, we have mostly been talking about intimacy in theory. What is it? Why is it important? How do we look at it and how can we apply it to your marriage? It's time to transform this theory into practice, so for each marker, I'll recommend some specific steps you can take to put that marker into practice.

As with any prescriptive marriage advice, you will have to tailor these instructions to suit your particular marriage. While these instructions will be helpful for most, every marriage is as distinct as the two individuals involved.

Trail Marker #1: The Magic Ratio

For some reason, many interactions between married couples seem to revolve around the negative. It's somewhat understandable. In real life, there are problems to be solved, schedules to be worked out, and issues to address. Negatives are natural.

The problem is that if most of your interactions are negative, it drains the life from your marriage—or worse.

Researchers at the Gottman Institute observed and recorded the positive and negative interactions of couples and then followed up with them nine years later. Based on what they observed, they were able to predict which couples would stay together and which would divorce with better than 90% accuracy. They determined that there is a magic ratio of positive to negative interactions which leads to lasting relationships. That "magic ratio" is 5-to-1. This means that for every negative interaction during conflict, a stable and happy marriage has five (or more) positive interactions. By contrast, for the couples who ended up divorced, the ratio was 0.8 to 1.[xv]

A similar report regarding the business world appeared in *Harvard Business Review*. One study found that for the highest performing teams, the average ratio of positive feedback to negative was 5.6 (that is, nearly six positive comments for every negative one). The medium-performance teams averaged 1.9 (almost twice as many positive comments than negative ones.) But the average for the low-performing teams, at 0.36 to 1, was almost three negative comments for every positive one.[xvi]

I don't know if there is actually a "magic number" or not, but the bottom line is that these two reports point to an important factor when it comes to keeping your marriage on the Path of Intimacy. Specifically, intimacy is fostered best when you develop the habit of positive interaction.

The Little Praise List, below, is a good place to start learning to speak positively to and about each other.

Another opportunity for positive interactions is to regularly and purposefully dream together. As we have discussed, transparency is an essential component of intimacy. It's the essence of being fully known. As important as being transparent with our weaknesses and mistakes is, I believe it is even more important to be transparent with our hopes, dreams, and ambitions. Transparency about the things that delight your heart gives your spouse a glimpse into what makes you tick.

My wife and I have, for years, taken the opportunity of our anniversary to try to paint a picture together of what we want our marriage to be like 5 or 10 years down the road. We also make a habit of sharing with each other our dreams and aspirations, which enables us to become partners in going after our goals.

Put it Into Practice:

Plan a date that is specifically for that purpose of dreaming together. This is not the time to talk about who will pick the kids up from soccer practice and other such mundane topics. Here are some questions you might consider asking each other:

- Describe what you want our marriage to be like in five years.
- If you could eliminate the risk of failure, what is one thing you would like to do that you have never done before?
- Is there someplace special you would like to visit?
- What would you do if you won ten million dollars in the lottery tomorrow?

Trail Marker #2: What's Your One Thing?

If you are going to get good at meeting each other's needs, you are going to have to get good at talking about them with each other.

The best way to begin that conversation is to ask each other the question I asked my readers about: "What is the one thing you need most from me right now?" I would suggest you spend some time before you talk thinking about it. Your answer is important. (If you feel a bit stuck, you can start with the results of my reader poll found in Chapter 5.)

There is a second and equally important question that we must also answer if the conversation is to be fruitful. "What would it look like to have that need fully satisfied?"

Put it into practice:

When you've both had time to consider these questions, set aside at least 30 minutes of uninterrupted time to talk about your answers.

Here are some important tips for this discussion:

- If you are comfortable praying together start with prayer. Ask the Holy Spirit to preside and to make this conversation fruitful for the benefit of growing intimacy between you.
- Listen without judgment. You don't get to decide what your spouse's needs are.
- Listen for issues of the heart. Discern the feelings or emotions involved and the impact this need has on him or her.
- Tune in completely. While your partner is speaking, it is time for listening, not for preparing your response. Focus.
- Parrot back what you hear your spouse saying to see if you have a good understanding. Keep going until the answer to "Do I understand it correctly" is an unequivocal "yes."

- While you are talking, focus on you. Don't accuse or blame your spouse.
- If things get heated, take a break.
- You may find it helpful to write down what your spouse reveals through the conversation. Keep your notes and refer to them regularly.

The "one thing" discussion is not a one-time event. I suggest you revisit it regularly. Seasons of marriage change and our needs tend to evolve with those seasons.

And while I think there is value on focusing on the "one thing" that is your highest need, some will find it helpful to consider additional needs, although I would suggest that happen in a later, separate conversation.

Trail Marker #3: Responding to Bids

Relationship researchers from the Gottman Institute developed the concept of emotional bids[xvii]. In essence, bids are attempts to gain attention, affirmation, affection, or some other positive connection from your spouse. Bids can be overt requests, such as asking for help with something, but more often than not they are subtler, such as sitting down next to your spouse or letting out a deep sigh.

Bids evoke one of three responses:

1. **Turn away** – ignore the bid and move on
2. **Turn against** – respond negatively to the bid (disrespect, defensiveness, anger, accusation)
3. **Turn toward** – respond with interest and affection

What the Gottman research showed is that the response to bids is also a reliable predictor of marital success. They found that the couples who were still married six years after their initial observations responded to bids by turning toward their partner 86% of the time. Those who were later found divorced only did so 33% of the time. That's an astounding difference, and it offers an important lesson. Paying attention to how you respond to bids from your spouse has a huge impact on the longevity of your marriage.

In many cases, turning toward your partner is not the easiest choice. It might require a little of your time and a bit of emotional or physical effort. However, the long-term benefit of building connection and trust is well worth the short-term sacrifice.

The trickiest part of emotional bids, however, is not in the choice of how to respond. No, the hardest part is actually realizing when they are happening. Some bids will be obvious, but many may be almost imperceptible.

Some examples of obvious bids:
- "How do I look in this?"
- "Can we talk?"
- "Do you want to come with me to the grocery store?"
- "Let's go fool around."

Some examples of more subtle bids:
- "Wow, what a day I had."
- A sigh, a frown, or staring blankly into space.

- Your spouse comes and sits close to you on the couch.
- "I've missed you lately."
- Silence.
- "I just don't know what to do."

Whether obvious or subtle, your response is critical for building trust in your relationship and keeping it on the Path of Intimacy.

You might say to yourself, "If he/she really needs something from me, why doesn't he/she just ask me?" First, it's quite possible that your spouse isn't even aware that he or she needs something. Second, when you respond to an unspoken desire for connection, you tell your spouse that you are tuned into them and eager to make a meaningful connection.

Put it Into Practice:

Spend an entire week being especially aware of emotional bids your spouse offers you, and make a commitment to respond by purposefully turning toward him or her. During the week, keep a journal of bids and of your specific responses and note how your response impacted your level of connection with your spouse.

Trail Marker #4: Little Love List

I tell couples all the time that little acts of love, expressed frequently and consistently, have a much greater impact on your marriage than grand gestures that only happen once in a while.

I recently heard a teaching on marriage by Kris Vallotton that included his story of a counseling session with a couple in a troubled marriage. At one point, they begin screaming at each other. The husband yelled, "I took you to Paris twice in four years!" The wife replied, "But you won't pick up your underwear!" Kris then interjected, "Whoa! Dude, you can't fix with a trip to Paris what you broke with your underwear." Kris then shared what he considers to be 75% of a great marriage: "Do what you do when you feel like, even when you don't." [xviii]

The point of the story is that it's easy to act lovingly and kindly toward our spouse when we feel like it. However, there will be plenty of times when you don't feel like it, either because of something your spouse has done or not done or because of external circumstances like stress or anxiety. Even in those times, we need to do the same things we do when we do feel like it.

The main trick to consistently doing the little things is to get yourself in the habit of doing them. The Little Love List is a tool I suggest couples use to help create a lifestyle of loving gestures. It is both simple and very effective.

For example, I frequently make tea for my wife, even though I'm not a tea drinker myself. And I often collect tea bags of various kinds when I travel abroad. She doesn't care for coffee but prepares my coffee in the evening for the next morning. When we wake up, we make sure we reach for each other before we reach for our phones and share a good morning kiss.

Put it Into Practice:

Either on a piece of paper (or on your phone or wherever you can keep it handy), make a short list of "little things" you know your husband or wife appreciates as expressions of love. Don't include "big things" that require major planning and time, but simple love expressions that you can easily incorporate on a daily basis. These may be things you've done before that you know make him or her feel loved or things that they have previously expressed as wishes.

In the coming few weeks, keep the list handy and incorporate at least a few of these things into your regular planning routine or specifically add them to your "to-do list." Spontaneity is great, but deliberate love is likely to be more consistently expressed. One trick that may be helpful is to think to yourself while you are doing your early morning routine about one thing you can do that day to bless your spouse.

You should take note of your spouse's responses as you work to refine your love list. What items have the biggest impact on your spouse or were received with the greatest enthusiasm? This kind of observation is part of learning to be a lifelong student of your spouse.

After a few weeks of practice, you might consider showing your love list to your spouse and ask for their feedback. Are there items on the list that your spouse doesn't care so much about? What are his or her favorites? What would your spouse add?

Trail Marker #5: Little Praise List

Words have power. They have the power to build up and the power to tear down.

I think too often in marriage, especially if we've been married a long time, we get in the habit of assuming that our spouse knows our thoughts. We don't feel the need to say things out loud that we feel are already known. Overcoming this habit is the purpose of the "little praise list."

The praise list is similar to the love list in that its purpose is to help you be intentional about saying things you appreciate about your spouse out loud on a regular basis.

Put it Into Practice:

Either on a piece of paper or on your phone (anywhere you can keep it handy), write down a dozen or so things you like about your spouse. In generating the list, here are some ideas to jog your thinking:

- What personality traits do you find most appealing?
- What physical attributes do you most admire? (Guys, don't go overboard here!)
- What kind things do they do for you? (Try to limit this to things that demonstrate your spouse's nature, because things they do for you

are really about you more than they are about your spouse).

- What positive spiritual attributes do they display?
- What kind of parent or child or friend are they?

Keep the list handy and read it every day. Add to it as you think of things. Learn to be aware of everything about your spouse that delights you.

As with the love list, it's a good idea to figure out how to make communicating your delight to your spouse part of your daily routine. Send a text. Leave a note. Say it in person. Whisper it in their ear after giving them an affectionate kiss or a long hug. Catch them doing what you've noted, and speak to it right away when you notice. Use a private communications app on your phones, such as Couple.

CHAPTER 9: A GRACE-FULL MARRIAGE

"The grace of God is greater than our sin or any other problem that we may have. You might be feeling guilty and tempted to shrink from God's presence, but He wants you to run to Him, not away from Him."[xix]

Joyce Meyer

Grace is one of the two most important tools for navigating the Path of Intimacy. (The second is watchfulness, which we will cover in the next chapter.) The first of these tools is grace.

The implications for grace in marriage are vast, just as they are in our walk with God. Grace is foundational. Without grace, no marriage can maintain intimacy and connection over the long haul.

Grace Is an Invitation to Intimacy

Grace keeps your marriage on the Path of Intimacy when other forces would knock you off.

Grace is nothing more—and nothing less—than unmerited favor, mercy, and kindness. It's easy to say but very hard to do. Because grace is one of God's most significant attributes, we would do well to mimic it in marriage. God's grace draws us near to Him in intimacy. It is His kindness that leads us to be transformed and renewed in the way we think and act, not His judgment or wrath (Romans 2:4).

Grace has the same power to transform your marriage.

"Grace? But wait," you say. "You don't know [my husband/wife]. You don't know what I put up with! He doesn't deserve it!"

Okay, I'll admit it, I don't. But here's the crazy thing about grace: God knew everything about you, every sin and weakness, every bad choice, and angry word and spiteful act you would ever commit, yet He chose to let His own Son, Jesus, be put to death so that He could have intimacy with you forever.

That is grace. *Ridiculous, extravagant grace. It is reckless mercy, and it is what we are called to duplicate in our marriage.*

"I'm not God," you reply.

Neither am I. I'm not anywhere near as good at this grace thing as God is. Nobody will ever be. But I know enough to realize that there is a promise in grace: that promise is intimacy. Grace is an invitation to intimacy.

Yes, our spouses are full of flaws and mistakes and at times will come out with unkind words and careless actions. As long as there are people involved in marriages, there will be pain. Plenty of it. Don't let the pain knock you off the Path of Intimacy. At least not for long.

For grace to be the norm in your marriage, you have to want intimacy more than you want perfection. Focus on being love more than on being right.

It's really that simple. I'm not saying it is easy. Quite the opposite, in fact. But I do know the power of grace is transformational. It's simply amazing.

Which Way Do You Run?

When you make a mess in your marriage, which way do you run? Do you turn away from your spouse to run and hide, making excuses and avoiding blame? Or do you turn toward your spouse with a sincere desire to make amends and re-establish your connection?

In the same way that shame and fear cause you to run from God, so too it is with your spouse. When you know you will receive love and grace in response to our missteps, it allows you to run toward your spouse, just as it does in your relationship with God.

Running away widens the gap between you at just the time when what you need most is to close the gap. Sure, it feels safer to distance yourself from the person you've offended, or who has hurt or offended you, but separation is never the solution. Intimacy is.

The next time you are tempted to take offense or to be offended, step back, take a breath, and ask yourself this question: "How can we best maintain our connection through this?" If intimacy is truly the highest goal of your marriage, then it is even more important than who is right and who is wrong.

Grace puts you and your spouse on the same team, against the problem or issue instead of against each other.

Grace says, "I am for you. I am for us. We can face this together."

Run toward your spouse—always.

Grace Is Contagious

The best way to ensure that your spouse extends grace to you when you've blown it is to work toward an atmosphere of grace in your marriage.

And the best way to fill your marriage with grace is to first experience the overwhelming and extravagant grace of God toward you and your spouse— to allow grace to have its full effect in your own life. Then, when your spouse messes up, make every effort to respond with that same grace and love.

Don't turn away in offense. Don't distance yourself in retribution. Reach out, extend grace, and strive to maintain intimacy through the trouble.

Grace is contagious! The more you extend grace, the more you shift the atmosphere of your marriage toward grace, and the more likely it is that you'll receive that same kind of grace when you need it. It's not a guarantee, of course, but it definitely improves the odds.

Be quick to forgive and eager to encourage as you grow together in this. Learn to communicate in positive and helpful ways, without accusation or condemnation.

The Fruit of Grace

Ask yourself this question: How different would your marriage be if you never, ever doubted your spouse's love for you? And suppose your spouse never, ever doubted that you truly love him or her? How delightful would your marriage be if you lived every moment in celebration of the secure love you share and never had to strive to earn love?

This the fruit of grace: confidence in love. Security, trust, and peace grow in a marriage filled with grace.

So, the next time you feel tempted to turn away and hide from your spouse because you've made a mess of things, stop yourself. The next time you want to react in anger or judgment, stop and choose to respond differently. Make a deliberate turn toward him or her. Trust in their love. Seek to maintain your connection while you work it through together.

Grace Loves "As If"

Finally, there is tremendous power to propel your marriage forward when you love each other "as if."

Because of the grace granted to us through Jesus, when God looks at us, He sees us in perfection. That's what grace does. It looks through the outward appearance and sees into the real person, as God intends them to be.

Loving your spouse "as if" assumes the best. It means we are willing to see each other from the perspective of heaven. It means believing that each has the best intentions for the other. It trusts in the love your spouse has for you. Believe "as if" love is at the center of all you do, even when it seems otherwise. Be generous and gracious in the giving and receiving of love, no matter what.

As you discover more and more about each other, grace fans the embers of intimacy into flame. Connection grows deeper as you learn to take absolute delight in what you see in one another. Yes, it is something you have to learn to do. Sometimes that will mean loving them in spite of their weakness. That's just how Jesus loves us. He loves us past our shortcoming and into what He sees us to be. He loves us "as if."

If you want the Path of Intimacy, choose the way of grace. Be extravagant in giving it and gracious in receiving it. It will do wonders for the intimacy in your marriage.

CHAPTER 10:
WATCHFULNESS –
SWITCHING OFF THE
AUTOPILOT

Devote yourselves to prayer,
being watchful and thankful.

Colossians 4:2

Watchfulness is not a concept that gets much attention these days. Maybe you've never heard of it—but it is the second important tool for navigating the Path of Intimacy. What Is Watchfulness?

Watchfulness amounts to taking yourself, your life, and your marriage off auto-pilot.

How do you do that? It starts with a determination to remain attentive and observant to all that goes on in and around you and your marriage, keeping your heart, mind, spirit, and physical senses alive and alert.

Being watchful in your marriage means purposefully and continually stirring your passions and longings for each other to keep your marriage squarely in the middle of the Path of Intimacy.

Watchfulness is a spiritual as well as a marital concept. Spiritual watchfulness means fostering a continual awareness of the presence of God in your life (even in the little things), living in anticipation of His goodness, and having your heart fully awake to His love. Choose to see God in everything: the smile of a child, the beauty of creation, and the tastiness of a meal. Know that He is always with us, both in the good times and in the challenges of life. Ultimately, watchfulness grows intimacy between God and us.

In your marriage, watchfulness has the similar ability to fuel intimacy and passion. By remaining aware of how the things you are thinking, feeling, saying, and doing affect your marriage, you create the opportunity to be intentional, to find meaning, to take positive action, and to encounter pleasure.

Other words I associate with the notion of watchfulness are observant, vigilant, sharp, heedful, careful, alert, wide-awake, alive, deliberate, intentional, purposeful, resolved, zealous, tuned-in, and attentive.

Like a Compass

Watchfulness is a compass for your journey along the Path of Intimacy. This compass helps you to ask and answer questions like:

- What can I do today to let my wife know I love her?
- Are these thoughts I keep having helping or hurting my relationship with my husband? Where do I need to change my thinking?
- Have I adequately put my feelings of love into affirming words this week?

- Am I doing ____ more for me or my spouse? Is that the right choice in this matter?
- During the fight we just had, did I show distrust or disrespect toward my husband in any way? What should I do about that?
- What bids has my spouse offered today? Have I responded by turning toward him or her?
- What kind of time have we invested in each other in the past day or two? Is it really enough, or are we just giving each other our leftovers?
- What have I done today to intentionally stir up my passion for my wife or my husband?
- What have I truly savored with my senses (sights, tastes, smells, or sounds) today?
- Have we truly talked this week about more than functional things? Have we gotten real about how we are and what we feel about what's happening lately?
- In our most recent disagreement, did I allow grace to be at the center of our conversation? Was I more focused on being right than on maintaining our connection?
- What do I sense that God is doing in our marriage these days? Have I communicated that to my spouse?

As you can see, watchfulness involves your whole being, meaning that you should try to stay attuned to your spirit, mind, emotions, and body, keeping them all intensively alive and alert for the sake of enhancing intimacy and passion in your marriage.

A Deeper Awareness

Are you thinking, "I don't have time for all of this?"

If so, then you are thinking about watchfulness in the wrong way. It is much more about how you *think* than what you *do*. Keeping your spirit, mind, emotions, and body alert and attentive is mainly an internal discipline—a mindset. Therefore, it can be difficult to quantify and even more difficult to master. Nonetheless, watchfulness can help inform your every action and attitude, guard every emotion, and guide every thought in your marriage relationship.

Watchfulness is a mindset and a habit of awareness much more than it is a checklist of dos and don'ts. In fact, this kind of checklist thinking is precisely what watchfulness is meant to preclude.

Watchfulness doesn't always have to mean extra physical effort. Sometimes it might just be a spark of awareness in your mind or body.

- While dressing for a date, think of an outfit that your spouse has complimented you on before or pick something that you know is his or her preference.
- As you splash on his favorite perfume or her favorite cologne, imagine the intoxicating impact it will have on your spouse when you embrace or as you crawl into bed together.

- Purposefully reflect on intimate and romantic moments you have shared together, allowing the same feelings of enjoyment to wash over you again.
- While sitting in traffic on the way home, think about how you want to greet your spouse when you walk in the door.
- When you step out of the shower, or when you are changing for bed, purposefully allow your spouse to enjoy your nakedness for a moment.

Watchfulness trains your mind to seek out pleasure and take delight even in the little things.

Watch Your Whole Marriage

Your marriage has many dimensions, and it is important not to let any of them fall prey to the auto-pilot syndrome.

For example, watching your spiritual relationship means making sure that Christ stays at the center of your life and your marriage. Watching your sexual relationship not only means making sex a priority but also being purposeful to keeping it interesting and exciting and to actively fuel passion for your spouse. Watching your financial relationship means things like being entirely transparent with your money and being diligent to stay within budget and saving guidelines. Watching your emotional relationship includes prioritizing dates and other one-on-one time.

There is a wonderful synergy that happens as you begin cultivating watchfulness throughout your marriage. As you practice awareness and anticipation in one area, say in your spiritual life, you may find yourself suddenly more able to do so in another area, maybe in your sexual relationship. When you become attentive to helping your spouse out in practical ways, you may find it easier also to be attentive to good communications.

Learn to be watchful over your entire marriage!

The Danger of Anesthetics

Many things around us anesthetize us against watchfulness and can lead us to quickly re-engage the autopilot.

- ***Busyness*** – Watchfulness is a call to do less and think and feel more.
- ***Media Overload*** – Turn off the TV, the Xbox, and the computer and just be.
- ***Social Media*** – Limit how often you "zone out" by endlessly cruising social media.
- ***Consumerism*** – Remember that less really can be more.

I could give you plenty more examples of things that we anesthetize our souls with. I'm sure you can readily identify the top two or three in your own life.

The danger of using these things to numb is that we can't numb selectively. When we anesthetize against the negative things in your life, we also numb pleasure, joy, and creativity.

Most dangerous of all, we also numb connection with our spouse.

Create Little Rituals of Pleasure

Practice taking delight and pleasure in the little things. One way to do this is to create small intentional "rituals" around things that we often do without thinking about them.

Here are some examples:

- Enjoy an after-dinner cup of tea or coffee in a quiet place together.
- Follow up your evening walk together with three minutes of kissing or hugging.
- Sip a glass of fine wine after work in a comfortable spot while watching the sunset.
- Light candles while you pray together for your family.
- Create a romantic or sexy playlist for lovemaking.
- Hold your monthly budget discussions in bed, naked.

What things do you do on a daily or semi-regular basis that you can modify slightly in a way that creates an enjoyable ritual out of it? The possibilities are truly endless!

CHAPTER 11:
CONCLUDING
THOUGHTS

The journey into deeper intimacy in your marriage is one every couple can and should take. It doesn't matter how long you've been married, how strong your marriage is or how close you currently are to your spouse; there is always more.

Remember, intimacy is the main goal of your marriage. Keeping that goal at the forefront of your relationship changes everything. Pursuing intimacy first and foremost is what allows you to let yourself be fully seen and experience a response based on unconditional love and grace.

When you watchfully avoid the things that put your marriage on the Path of Separation and actively pursue the Path of Intimacy, you prevent you and your spouse from devolving into "excellent roommates." What's more, you fan the flames of love and passion in ways that make your marriage a delight.

I hope you'll accept my challenge to ignite or reignite the intimacy in your marriage and set your relationship firmly on the Path of Intimacy.

ABOUT THE AUTHOR

As a champion for great marriages, Scott Means has been writing and teaching about the passion and intimacy found in God's design for marriage for more than ten years. His mantra is "Marriage was God's idea, so let's do it His way." As a blogger, encourager, mentor, teacher, and author, Scott has impacted thousands of marriages through his blog, books, and other marriage resources.

Whether your marriage is missing the spark it once had or you just want it to be great rather than good, Scott's insights help any couple down the path of true intimacy toward a deeply passionate and joyfully enduring marriage.

While exploring the beautiful intersection of the spiritual and marital, Scott brings these concepts down to earth, offering practical tips and techniques while challenging you to change the way you see your marriage. He pushes back against many of the common marriage paradigms found through secular wisdom, placing them in sharp contrast the wisdom found in biblical marriage paradigms.

Scott Means will challenge, provoke, inform and, most of all, equip and motivate you to attain the intimacy, passion, and love you've always dreamed of in your marriage.
Scott is the founder of HMM Creations, LLC.

Visit his website:
https://www.HeavenMadeMarriage.com

On Facebook:
https://www.facebook.com/HeavenMadeMarriage

Twitter: @MarriageJourney

Instagram: @HeavenMadeMarriage

Keep up with Scott's new releases.
Join his Resources mailing list.
https://www.heavenmademarriage.com/resources

NOTES

Chapter 1

[i] Brown, Brene. Daring Greatly: How the Courage to Be Vulnerable Transforms the Way We Live, Love, Parent, and Lead. Penguin Life, 2015.

Chapter 2

[ii] New King James Version (NKJV) Scripture taken from the New King James Version®. Copyright © 1982 by Thomas Nelson. Used by permission. All rights reserved.

[iii] Intimacy, s.v. "Intimacy," accessed December 3, 2017, http://www.dictionary.com/browse/intimacy.

[iv] Journey to Surrender (2016, March 8) Discover True Intimacy [Blog post] (http://www.surrenderedmarriage.org/2016/03/discover-true-intimacy.html

Chapter 3

[v] Simmons, Brian. John: Eternal Love (The Passion Translation) (Kindle Locations 1284-1285). BroadStreet Publishing Group LLC. Kindle Edition.

[vi] Miller, Donald. Scary Close: Dropping the Act and Finding True Intimacy (p. 188). Thomas Nelson. Kindle Edition.

[vii] Kathleen Deveny, "We're Not in the Mood," Newsweek, June 29, 2003, http://www.newsweek.com/were-not-mood-138387.

Chapter 4

[viii] New King James Version®. Copyright © 1982 by Thomas Nelson. Used by permission. All rights reserved.

Chapter 5

[ix] THE MESSAGE, copyright © 1993, 1994, 1995, 1996, 2000, 2001, 2002 by Eugene H. Peterson. Used by permission of NavPress. All rights reserved. Represented by Tyndale House Publishers, Inc.

[x] New King James Version®. Copyright © 1982 by Thomas Nelson. Used by permission. All rights reserved.

Chapter 6

[xi] J Parker, "Man vs. Woman: The Differences," Hot, Holy & Humorous (blog), February 23, 2012, http://hotholyhumorous.com/2012/02/man-vs-woman/.

[xii] Gregory L. Jantz, "Brain Differences Between Genders," Psychology Today, February 27, 2014, https://www.psychologytoday.com/blog/hope-relationships/201402/brain-differences-between-genders

Chapter 7

[xiii] Jonathan David Helser, "Beautiful Surrender," https://bethelmusic.com/albums/beautiful-surrender/

Chapter 8

[xiv] Frank A. Clark, https://www.quotes.net/quote/11983

[xv] Kyle Benson, "The Magic Relationship Ratio, According to Science," The Gottman Institute Blog, October 4, 2017, https://www.gottman.com/blog/the-magic-relationship-ratio-according-science/

[xvi] Jack Zenger and Joseph Folkman, "The Ideal Praise-to-Criticism Ratio," Harvard Business Review, March 15, 2013, https://hbr.org/2013/03/the-ideal-praise-to-criticism.

[xvii] Lisitsa, Ellie "An Introduction to Emotional Bids and Trust" The Gottman Institute Blog, August 31, 2012, https://www.gottman.com/blog/an-introduction-to-emotional-bids-and-trust/

[xviii] Bethel Church, Redding's Facebook page, accessed January 6, 2018, https://www.facebook.com/bethel.church.redding/videos/10154807527226824/

Chapter 9

[xix] Meyer, Joyce. Closer to God Each Day: 365 Devotions for everyday living. Kindle, Faith Words, 2015

33076432R00054

Made in the USA
Columbia, SC
07 November 2018